BLACK LEGACY PRESS™

WWW.BLACKLEGACYPRESS.ORG

The mule-bone
a comedy of Negro life in three acts
By
Langston Hughes
Zora Neale Hurston

ISBN: 978-1-63652-348-4

THE MULE-BONE

A COMEDY OF NEGRO LIFE IN THREE ACTS

LANGSTON HUGHES
ZORA NEALE HURSTON

CONTENTS

CHARACTERS

JIM WESTON: Guitarist, Methodist, slightly arrogant, agressive, somewhat self-important, ready with his tongue.

DAVE CARTER: Dancer, Baptist, soft, happy-go-lucky character, slightly dumb and unable to talk rapidly and wittily.

DAISY TAYLOR.

Methodist, domestic servant, plump, dark and sexy, self-conscious of clothes and appeal, fickle.

JOE CLARK.

The Mayor, storekeeper and postmaster, arrogant, ignorant and powerful in a self-assertive way, large, fat man, Methodist.

ELDER SIMMS.

Methodist minister, newcomer in town, ambitious, small and fly, but not very intelligent.

ELDER CHILDERS.

Big, loose-jointed, slow spoken but not dumb. Long resident in the town, calm and sure of himself.

KATIE CARTER: Dave's aunt, little old wizened dried-up lady.

MRS. HATTIE CLARK.

The Mayor's wife, fat and flabby mulatto high-pitched voice.

THE MRS. REV. SIMMS.

Large and agressive.

THE MRS. REV. CHILDERS.

Just a wife who thinks of details.

LUM BOGER.

Young town marshall about twenty, tall, gangly, with big flat feet, liked to show off in public.

TEET MILLER: Village vamp who is jealous of DAISY.

LIGE MOSELY: A village wag.

WALTER THOMAS.

Another village wag.

ADA LEWIS: A promiscuous lover.

DELLA LEWIS: Baptist, poor housekeeper, mother of ADA.

BOOTSIE PITTS: A local vamp.

MRS. DILCIE ANDERSON: Village housewife, Methodist.

WILLIE NIXON.

Methodist, short runt.

ACT ONE

SETTING: The raised porch of JOE CLARK'S Store and the street in front. Porch stretches almost completely across the stage, with a plank bench at either end. At the center of the porch three steps leading from street. Rear of porch, center, door to the store. On either side are single windows on which signs, at left, "POST OFFICE", and at right, "GENERAL STORE" are painted. Soap boxes, axe handles, small kegs, etc., on porch on which townspeople sit and lounge during action. Above the roof of the porch the "false front", or imitation second story of the shop is seen with large sign painted across it "JOE CLARK'S GENERAL STORE". Large kerosine street lamp on post at right in front of porch.

Saturday afternoon and the villagers are gathered around the store. Several men sitting on boxes at edge of porch chewing sugar cane, spitting tobacco juice, arguing, some whittling, others eating peanuts. During the act the women all dressed up in starched dresses parade in and out of store. People buying groceries, kids playing in the street, etc. General noise of conversation, laughter and children shouting. But when the curtain rises there is momentary lull for cane-chewing. At left of porch four men are playing cards on a soap box, and seated on the edge of the porch at extreme right two children are engaged in a checker game, with the board on the floor between them.

When the curtain goes up the following characters are discovered on the porch: MAYOR JOE CLARK, the storekeeper; DEACON HAMBO; DEACON GOODWIN; Old Man MATT BRAZZLE; WILL CODY; SYKES JONES; LUM BOGER, the young town

3

marshall; LIGE MOSELY and WALTER THOMAS, two village wags; TOM NIXON and SAM MOSELY, and several others, seated on boxes, kegs, benches and floor of the porch. TONY TAYLOR is sitting on steps of porch with empty basket. MRS. TAYLOR comes out with her arms full of groceries, empties them into basket and goes back in store. All the men are chewing sugar cane earnestly with varying facial expressions. The noise of the breaking and sucking of cane can be clearly heard in the silence. Occasionally the laughter and shouting of children is heard nearby off stage.

HAMBO.

(To BRAZZLE) Say, Matt, gimme a jint or two of dat green cane—dis ribbon cane is hard.

LIGE.

Yeah, and you ain't got de chears in yo' parlor you useter have.

HAMBO.

Dat's all right, Lige, but I betcha right now wid dese few teeth I got I kin eat up more cane'n you kin grow.

LIGE.

I know you kin and that's de reason I ain't going to tempt you. But youse gettin' old in lots of ways—look at dat bald-head—just as clean as my hand. (Exposes his palm).

HAMBO.

Don't keer if it tis—I don't want nothin'—not even hair—between me and God. (General laughter—LIGE joins in as well. Cane chewing keeps up. Silence for a moment.)

(Off stage a high shrill voice can be heard calling:)

4

VOICE.

Sister Mosely, Oh, Sister Mosely! (A pause) Miz Mosely! (Very irritated) Oh, Sister Mattie! You hear me out here—you just won't answer!

VOICE OF MRS. MOSELY.

Whoo-ee ... somebody calling me?

VOICE OF MRS. ROBERTS.

(Angrily) Never mind now—you couldn't come when I called you. I don't want yo' lil ole weasley turnip greens. (Silence)

MATT BRAZZLE.

Sister Roberts is en town agin! If she was mine, I'll be hen-fired if I wouldn't break her down in de lines (loins)—good as dat man is to her!

HAMBO.

I wish she was mine jes' one day—de first time she open her mouf to beg *anybody*, I'd lam her wid lightning.

JOE CLARK.

I God, Jake Roberts buys mo' rations out dis store than any man in dis town. I don't see to my Maker whut she do wid it all.... Here she come....

(ENTER MRS. JAKE ROBERTS, a heavy light brown woman with a basket on her arm. A boy about ten walks beside her carrying a small child about a year old straddle of his back. Her skirts are sweeping the ground. She walks up to the step, puts one foot upon the steps and looks forlornly at all the men, then fixes her look on JOE CLARK.)

MRS. ROBERTS.

Evenin', Brother Mayor.

CLARK.

Howdy do, Mrs. Roberts. How's yo' husband?

MRS. ROBERTS.

(Beginning her professional whine): He ain't much and I ain't much and my chillun is poly. We ain't got 'nough to eat! Lawd, Mr. Clark, gimme a lil piece of side meat to cook us a pot of greens.

CLARK.

Aw gwan, Sister Roberts. You got plenty bacon home. Last week Jake bought....

MRS. ROBERTS.

(Frantically) Lawd, Mist' Clark, how long you think dat lil piece of meat last me an' my chillun? Lawd, me and my chillun is *hongry*! God knows, Jake don't fee-eed me!

(MR. CLARK sits unmoved. MRS. ROBERTS advances upon him)

Mist' Clark!

CLARK.

I God, woman, don't keep on after me! Every time I look, youse round here beggin' for everything you see.

LIGE.

And whut she don't see she whoops for it just de same.

MRS. ROBERTS.

(In dramatic begging pose) Mist' Clark! Ain't you boin' do nuthin' for me? And you see me and my poor chillun is starvin'....

CLARK.

(Exasperated rises) I God, woman, a man can't git no peace wid somebody like you in town. (He goes angrily into the store followed by MRS. ROBERTS. The boy sits down on the edge of the porch sucking the baby's thumb.)

VOICE OF MRS. ROBERTS.

A piece 'bout dis wide....

VOICE OF CLARK.

I God, naw! Yo' husband done bought you plenty meat, nohow.

VOICE OF MRS. ROBERTS.

(In great anguish) Ow! Mist' Clark! Don't you cut dat lil tee-ninchy piece of meat for me and my chillun! (Sound of running feet inside the store.) I ain't a going to tetch it!

VOICE OF CLARK.

Well, don't touch it then. That's all you'll git outa me.

VOICE OF MRS. ROBERTS.

(Calmer) Well, hand it chear den. Lawd, me and my chillun is *so* hongry.... Jake don't fee-eed me. (She re-enters by door of store with the slab of meat in her hand and an outraged look on her face. She gazes all about her for sympathy.) Lawd, me and my poor chillun is *so* hongry ... and some folks has _every_thing and they's so *stingy* and gripin'.... Lawd knows, Jake don't fee-eed me! (She exits right on this line followed by the boy with the baby on his back.)

(All the men gaze behind her, then at each other and shake their heads.)

HAMBO.

Poor Jake. I'm really sorry for dat man. If she was mine I'd beat her till her ears hung down like a Georgy mule.

WALTER THOMAS.

I'd beat her till she smell like onions.

LIGE.

I'd romp on her till she slack like lime.

NIXON.

I'd stomp her till she rope like okra.

VOICE OF MRS. ROBERTS.

(Off stage right) Lawd, Miz Lewis, you goin' give me dat lil han'ful of greens for me and my chillun. Why dat ain't a eye-full. I ought not to take 'em … but me and my chillun is *so* hongry…. Some folks is so stingy and gripin'! Lawd knows, Tony don't *feed* me!

(The noise of cane-chewing is heard again. Enter JOE LINDSAY left with a gun over his shoulder and the large leg bone of a mule in the other hand. He approaches the step wearily.)

HAMBO.

Well, did you git any partridges, Joe?

JOE.

(Resting his gun and seating himself) Nope, but I made de feathers fly.

HAMBO.

I don't see no birds.

JOE.

Oh, the feathers flew off on de birds.

LIGE.

I don't see nothin' but dat bone. Look lak you done kilt a cow and et 'im raw out in de woods.

JOE.

Don't y'all know dat hock-bone?

WALTER.

How you reckon we gointer know every hock-bone in Orange County sight unseen?

JOE.

(Standing the bone up on the floor of the porch) Dis is a hock-bone of Brazzle's ole yaller mule.

(General pleased interest. Everybody wants to touch it.)

BRAZZLE.

(Coming forward) Well, sir! (Takes bone in both hands and looks up and down the length of it) If 'tain't my ole mule! This sho was one hell of a mule, too. He'd fight every inch in front of de plow … he'd turn over de mowing machine … run away wid de wagon … and you better not look like you wanter *ride* 'im!

LINDSAY.

(Laughing) Yeah, I 'member seein' you comin' down de road just so … (He limps wid one hand on his buttocks) one day.

BRAZZLE.

Dis mule was so evil he used to try to bite and kick when I'd go in de stable to feed 'im.

WALTER.

He was too mean to git fat. He was so skinny you could do a

9

week's washing on his ribs for a washboard and hang 'em up on his hip-bones to dry.

LIGE.

I 'member one day, Brazzle, you sent yo' boy to Winter Park after some groceries wid a basket. So here he went down de road ridin' dis mule wid dis basket on his arm…. Whut you reckon dat ole contrary mule done when he got to dat crooked place in de road going round Park Lake? He turnt right round and went through de handle of dat basket … wid de boy still up on his back. (General laughter)

BRAZZLE.

Yeah, he up and died one Sat'day just for spite … but he was too contrary to lay down on his side like a mule orter and die decent. Naw, he made out to lay down on his narrer contracted back and die wid his feets sticking straight up in de air just so. (He gets down on his back and illustrates.) We drug him out to de swamp wid 'im dat way, didn't we, Hambo?

JOE CLARK.

I God, Brazzle, we all seen it. Didn't we all go to de draggin' out? More folks went to yo' mule's draggin' out than went to last school closing…. Bet there ain't been a thing right in mule-hell for four years.

HAMBO.

Been dat long since he been dead?

CLARK.

I God, yes. He died de week after I started to cuttin' dat new ground.

(The bone is passing from hand to hand. At last a boy about twelve takes it. He has just walked up and is proudly handling the bone when a woman's voice is heard off stage right.)

VOICE.

Senator! Senator!! Oh, you Senator?

BOY.

(Turning displeased mutters) Aw, shux. (Loudly) Ma'm?

VOICE.

If you don't come here you better!

SENATOR.

Yes ma'am. (He drops bone on ground down stage and trots off frowning.) Soon as we men git to doing something dese wimmen…. (Exits, right.)

(Enter TEET and BOOTSIE left, clean and primped in voile dresses just alike. They speak diffidently and enter store. The men admire them casually.)

LIGE.

Them girls done turned out to be right good-looking.

WALTER.

Teet ain't as pretty now as she was a few years back. She used to be fat as a butter ball wid legs just like two whiskey-kegs. She's too skinny since she got her growth.

CODY.

Ain't none of 'em pretty as dat Miss Daisy. God! She's pretty as a speckled pup.

LIGE.

But she was sho nuff ugly when she was little … little ole hard black knot. She sho has changed since she been away up North. If she ain't pretty now, there ain't a hound dog in Georgy.

(Re-enter SENATOR BAILEY and stops on the steps. He addresses JOE CLARK.)

SENATOR.

Mist' Clark....

HAMBO.

(To Senator) Ain't you got no manners? We all didn't sleep wid you last night.

SENATOR.

(Embarrassed) Good evening, everybody.

ALL THE MEN.

Good evening, son, boy, Senator, etc.

SENATOR.

Mist' Clark, mama said is Daisy been here dis evenin'?

JOE CLARK.

Ain't laid my eyes on her. Ain't she working over in Maitland?

SENATOR.

Yessuh ... but she's off today and mama sent her down here to get de groceries.

JOE CLARK.

Well, tell yo' ma I ain't seen her.

SENATOR.

Well, she say to tell you when she come, to tell her ma say she better git home and dat quick.

JOE CLARK.

I will. (Exit BOY right.)

LIGE.

Bet she's off somewhere wid Dave or Jim.

WALTER.

I don't bet it ... I know it. She's got them two in de go-long.

(Re-enter TEET and BOOTSIE from store. TEET has a letter and BOOTSIE two or three small parcels. The men look up with interest as they come out on the porch.)

WALTER.

(Winking) Whut's dat you got, Teet ... letter from Dave?

TEET.

(Flouncing) Naw indeed! It's a letter from my B-I-T-sweetie! (Rolls her eyes and hips.)

WALTER.

(Winking) Well, ain't Dave yo' B-I-T-sweetie? I thought y'all was 'bout to git married. Everywhere I looked dis summer 'twas you and Dave, Bootsie and Jim. I thought all of y'all would've done jumped over de broomstick by now.

TEET.

(Flourishing letter) Don't tell it to me ... tell it to the ever-loving Mr. Albert Johnson way over in Apopka.

BOOTSIE.

(Rolling her eyes) Oh, tell 'em 'bout the ever-loving Mr. Jimmy Cox from Altamont. Oh, I can't stand to see my baby lose.

HAMBO.

It's lucky y'all girls done got some more fellers, cause look like Daisy done treed both Jim and Dave at once, or they done treed here one.

TEET.

Let her have 'em ... nobody don't keer. They don't handle de "In God we trust" lak my Johnson. He's head bellman at de hotel.

BOOTSIE.

Mr. Cox got money's grandma and old grandpa change. (The girls exit huffily.)

LINDSAY.

(To HAMBO, pseudo-seriously) You oughtn't tease dem gals lak dat.

HAMBO.

Oh, I laks to see gals all mad. But dem boys is crazy sho nuff. Before Daisy come back here they both had a good-looking gal a piece. Now they 'bout to fall out and fight over half a gal a piece. Neither one won't give over and let de other one have her.

LIGE.

And she ain't thinking too much 'bout no one man. (Looks off left.) Here she come now. God! She got a mean walk on her!

WALTER.

Yeah, man. She handles a lot of traffic! Oh, mama, throw it in de river ... papa'll come git it!

LINDSAY.

Aw, shut up, you married men!

LIGE.

Man don't go blind cause he gits married, do he? (Enter DAISY hurriedly. Stops at step a moment. She is dressed in sheer organdie, white shoes and stockings.)

DAISY.

Good evening, everybody. (Walks up on the porch.)

ALL THE MEN.

(Very pleasantly) Good evening, Miss Daisy.

DAISY.

(To CLARK) Mama sent me after some meal and flour and some bacon and sausage oil.

CLARK.

Senator been here long time ago hunting you.

DAISY.

(Frightened) Did he? Oo … Mist' Clark, hurry up and fix it for me. (She starts on in the store.)

LINDSAY.

(Giving her his seat) You better wait here, Daisy.

(WALTER kicks LIGE to call his attention to LINDSAY'S attitude)

It's powerful hot in dat store. Lemme run fetch 'em out to you.

LIGE.

(To LINDSAY) *Run!* Joe Lindsay, you ain't been able to run since de big bell rung. Look at dat gray beard.

LINDSAY.

Thank God, I ain't gray all over. I'm just as good a man right now as any of you young 'uns. (He hurries on into the store.)

WALTER.

Daisy, where's yo' two body guards? It don't look natural to see you thout nary one of 'em.

DAISY.

(Archly) I ain't got no body guards. I don't know what you talkin' about.

LIGE.

Aw, don' try to come dat over us, Daisy. You know who we talkin' 'bout all right ... but if you want me to come out flat footed ... where's Jim and Dave?

DAISY.

Ain't they playin' somewhere for de white folks?

LIGE.

(To WALTER) Will you listen at dis gal, Walter? (To DAISY) When I ain't been long seen you and Dave going down to de Lake.

DAISY.

(Frightened) Don't y'all run tell mama where I been.

WALTER.

Well, you tell us which one you laks de best and we'll wipe our mouf (Gesture) and say nothin'. Dem boys been de best of friends all they life, till both of 'em took after you ... then good-bye, Katy bar de door!

DAISY.

(Affected innocence) Ain't they still playin' and dancin' together?

LIGE.

Yeah, but that's 'bout all they do 'gree on these days. That's de way it is wid men, young and old.... I don't keer how long they been friends and how thick they been ... a woman kin come between 'em. David and Jonather never would have been friends so long if Jonather had of been any great hand wid de wimmen. You ain't never seen no two roosters that likes one another.

DAISY.

I ain't tried to break 'em up.

WALTER.

Course you ain't. You don't have to. All two boys need to do is to git stuck on de same girl and they done broke up ... *right now!* Wimmen is something can't be divided equal.

(Re-enter JOE LINDSAY and CLARK with the groceries. DAISY jumps up and grabs the packages.)

LIGE.

(To DAISY) Want some of us ... me ... to go long and tote yo' things for you?

DAISY.

(Nervously) Naw, mama is riding her high horse today. Long as I been gone it wouldn't do for me to come walking up wid nobody. (She exits hurriedly right.)

(All the men watch her out of sight in silence.)

CLARK.

(Sighing) I God, know whut Daisy puts me in de mind of?

HAMBO.

No, what? (They all lean together.)

CLARK.

I God, a great big mango ... a sweet smell, you know, with a strong flavor, but not something you could mash up like a strawberry. Something with a body to it.

(General laughter, but not obscene.)

HAMBO.

(Admiringly) Joe Clark! I didn't know you had it in you!

(MRS. CLARK enters from store door and they all straighten up guiltily)

CLARK.

(Angrily to his wife) Now whut do you want? I God, the minute I set down, here you come....

MRS. CLARK.

Somebody want a stamp, Jody. You know you don't 'low me to bove wid de post office. (HE rises sullenly and goes inside the store.)

BRAZZLE.

Say, Hambo, I didn't see you at our Sunday School picnic.

HAMBO.

(Slicing some plug-cut tobacco) Nope, wan't there dis time.

WALTER.

Looka here, Hambo. Y'all Baptist carry dis close-communion business too far. If a person ain't half drownded in de lake and half et up by alligators, y'all think he ain't baptized, so you can't take communion wid him. Now I reckon you can't even drink lemonade and eat chicken perlow wid us.

HAMBO.

My Lord, boy, youse just *full* of words. Now, in de first place, if this year's picnic was lak de one y'all had last year … you ain't had no lemonade for us Baptists to turn down. You had a big ole barrel of rain water wid about a pound of sugar in it and one lemon cut up over de top of it.

LIGE.

Man, you sho kin mold 'em!

WALTER.

Well, I went to de Baptist picnic wid my mouf all set to eat chicken, when lo and behold y'all had chitlings! Do Jesus!

LINDSAY.

Hold on there a minute. There was plenty chicken at dat picnic, which I do know is right.

WALTER.

Only chicken I seen was half a chicken yo' pastor musta tried to swaller whole cause he was choked stiff as a board when I come long … wid de whole deacon's board beating him in de back, trying to knock it out his throat.

LIGE.

Say, dat puts me in de mind of a Baptist brother that was crazy 'bout de preachers and de preacher was crazy 'bout feeding his face. So his son got tired of trying to beat dese stump-knockers to de grub on the table, so one day he throwed out some slams 'bout dese preachers. Dat made his old man mad, so he tole his son to git out. He boy ast him "Where must I go, papa?" He says, "Go on to hell I reckon … I don't keer where you go."

So de boy left and was gone seven years. He come back one cold, windy night and rapped on de door. "Who dat?" de old man ast him. "It's me, Jack." De old man opened de door, so glad to see his son agin, and tole Jack to come in. He did and looked all round de place. Seven or eight preachers was sitting round de fire eatin' and drinkin'.

"Where you been all dis time, Jack?" de old man ast him.

"I been to hell," Jack tole him.

"Tell us how it is down there, Jack."

"Well," he says, "It's just like it is here ... you cain't git to de fire for de preachers."

HAMBO.

Boy, you kin lie just like de cross-ties from Jacksonville to Key West. De presidin' elder must come round on his circuit teaching y'all how to tell 'em, cause you couldn't lie dat good just natural.

WALTER.

Can't nobody beat Baptist folks lying ... and I ain't never found out how come you think youse so important.

LINDSAY.

Ain't we got de finest and de biggest church? Macedonia Baptist will hold more folks than any two buildings in town.

LIGE.

Thass right, y'all got a heap more church than you got members to go in it.

HAMBO.

Thass all right ... y'all ain't got neither de church nor de members. Everything that's had in this town got to be held in our church.

(Re-enter JOE CLARK.)

CLARK.

What you-all talkin'?

HAMBO.

Come on out, Tush Hawg, lemme beat you some checkers. I'm tired of fending and proving wid dese boys ain't got no hair on they chest yet.

CLARK.

I God, you mean you gointer get beat. You can't handle me … I'm a tush hawg.

HAMBO.

Well, I'm going to draw dem tushes right now. (To two small boys using checker board on edge of porch.) Here you chilluns, let de Mayor and me have that board. Go on out an' play an' give us grown folks a little peace. (The children go down stage and call out:)

SMALL BOY.

Hey, Senator. Hey, Marthy. Come on let's play chick-me, chick-me, cranie-crow.

CHILD'S VOICE.

(Off stage) All right! Come on, Jessie! (Enter several children, led by SENATOR, and a game begins in front of the store as JOE CLARK and HAMBO play checkers.)

JOE CLARK.

I God! Hambo, you can't play no checkers.

HAMBO.

(As they seat themselves at the check board) Aw, man, if you wasn't de Mayor I'd beat you all de time.

(The children get louder and louder, drowning out the men's voices.)

SMALL GIRL.

I'm gointer be de hen.

BOY.

And I'm gointer be de hawk. Lemme git maself a stick to mark wid.

(The boy who is the hawk squats center stage with a short twig in his hand. The largest girl lines up the other children behind her.)

GIRL.

(Mother Hen) (Looking back over her flock): Y'all ketch holt of one 'Nother's clothes so de hawk can't git yuh. (They do.) You all straight now?

CHILDREN.

Yeah. (The march around the hawk commences.)

HEN AND CHICKS:

Chick mah chick mah craney crow

Went to de well to wash ma toe

When I come back ma chick was gone

What time, ole witch?

HAWK.

(Making a tally on the ground) One!

HEN AND CHICKS.

(Repeat song and march.)

HAWK.

(Scoring again) Two!

(Can be repeated any number of times.)

HAWK.

Four. (He rises and imitates a hawk flying and trying to catch a chicken. Calling in a high voice:) Chickee.

HEN.

(Flapping wings to protect her young) My chickens sleep.

HAWK.

Chickee. (During all this the hawk is feinting and darting in his efforts to catch a chicken, and the chickens are dancing defensively, the hen trying to protect them.)

HEN.

My chicken's sleep.

HAWK.

I shall have a chick.

HEN.

You shan't have a chick.

HAWK.

I'm goin' home. (Flies off)

HEN.

Dere's de road.

HAWK.

My pot's a boilin'.

HEN.

Let it boil.

HAWK.

My guts a growlin'.

HEN.

Let 'em growl.

HAWK.

I must have a chick.

HEN.

You shan't have n'airn.

HAWK.

My mama's sick.

HEN.

Let her die.

HAWK.

Chickie!

HEN.

My chicken's sleep.

(HAWK darts quickly around the hen and grabs a chicken and leads him off and places his captive on his knees at the store porch. After a brief bit of dancing he catches another, then a third, etc.)

HAMBO.

(At the checker board, his voice rising above the noise of the playing children, slapping his sides jubilantly) Ha! Ha! I got you now. Go ahead on and move, Joe Clark ... jus' go ahead on and move.

LOUNGERS.

(Standing around two checker players) Ol' Deacon's got you now.

ANOTHER VOICE.

Don't see how he can beat the Mayor like that.

ANOTHER VOICE.

Got him in the Louisville loop. (These remarks are drowned by the laughter of the playing children directly in front of the porch. MAYOR JOE CLARK disturbed in his concentration on the checkers and peeved at being beaten suddenly turns toward the children, throwing up his hands.)

CLARK.

Get on 'way from here, you limbs of Satan, making all that racket so a man can't hear his ears. Go on, go on!

(THE MAYOR looks about excitedly for the town marshall. Seeing him playing cards on the other side of porch, he bellows:)

Lum Boger, whyn't you git these kids away from here! What kind of a marshall is you? All this passle of young'uns around here under grown people's feet, creatin' disorder in front of my store.

(LUM BOGER puts his cards down lazily, comes down stage and scatters the children away. One saucy little girl refuses to move.)

LUM BOGER.

Why'nt you go on away from here, Matilda? Didn't you hear me tell you-all to move?

LITTLE MATILDA.

(Defiantly) I ain't goin' nowhere. You ain't none of my mama. (Jerking herself free from him as LUM touches her.) My mama in the store and she told me to wait out here. So take that, ol' Lum.

LUM BOGER.

You impudent little huzzy, you! You must smell yourself ... youse so fresh.

MATILDA.

The wind musta changed and you smell your own top lip.

LUM BOGER.

Don't make me have to grab you and take you down a buttonhole lower.

MATILDA.

(Switching her little head) Go ahead on and grab me. You sho can't kill me, and if you kill me, you sho can't eat me. (She marches into the store.)

SENATOR.

(Derisively from behind stump) Ol' dumb Lum! Hey! Hey!

(LITTLE BOY at edge of stage thumbs his nose at the marshall.)

(LUM lumbers after the small boy. Both exit.)

HAMBO.

(To CLARK who has been thinking all this while what move to make) You ain't got but one move ... go ahead on and make it. What's de matter, Mayor?

CLARK.

(Moving his checker) Aw, here.

HAMBO.

(Triumphant) Now! Look at him, boys. I'm gonna laugh in notes. (Laughing to the scale and jumping a checker each time) Do, sol, fa, me, lo … one! (Jumping another checker) La, sol, fa, me, do … two! (Another jump.) Do, sol, re, me, lo … three! (Jumping a third.) Lo, sol, fa, me, re … four! (The crowd begins to roar with laughter. LUM BOGER returns, looking on. Children come drifting back again playing chick-me-chick-me-cranie crow.)

VOICE.

Oh, ha! Done got the ol' tush hog.

ANOTHER VOICE.

Thought you couldn't be beat, Brother Mayor?

CLARK.

(Peeved, gets up and goes into the store mumbling) Oh, I coulda beat you if I didn't have this store on my mind. Saturday afternoon and I got work to do. Lum, ain't I told you to keep them kids from playin' right in front of this store?

(LUM makes a pass at the nearest half-grown boy. The kids dart around him teasingly.)

ANOTHER VOICE.

Eh, heh…. Hambo done run him on his store … done run the ol' coon in his hole.

ANOTHER VOICE.

That ain't good politics, Hambo, beatin' the Mayor.

ANOTHER VOICE.

Well, Hambo, you don't got to be so hard at checkers, come on let's see what you can do with de cards. Lum Boger there got his hands full nursin' the chilluns.

ANOTHER VOICE.

(At the table) We ain't playin' for money, nohow, Deacon. We just playin' a little Florida Flip.

HAMBO.

Ya all can't play no Florida Flip. When I was a sinner there wasn't a man in this state could beat me playin' that game. But I'm a deacon in Macedonia Baptist now and I don't bother with the cards no more.

VOICE AT CARD TABLE.

All right, then, come on here Tony (To man with basket on steps.) let me catch your jack.

TAYLOR.

(Looking toward door) I don't reckon I got time. I guess my wife gonna get through buying out that store some time or other and want to go home.

OLD MAN.

(On opposite side of porch from card game) I bet my wife would know better than expect me to sit around and wait for her with a basket. Whyn't you tell her to tote it on home herself?

TAYLOR.

(Sighing and shaking his head.) Eh, Lawd!

VOICE AT CARD TABLE.

Look like we can't get nobody to come into this game. Seem like everybody's scared a us. Come on back here, Lum, and take your hand. (LUM makes a final futile gesture at the children.)

LUM.

Ain't I tole you little haitians to stay away from here?

(CHILDREN scatter teasingly only to return to their play in front of the store later on. LUM comes up on the porch and re-joins the card game. Just as he gets seated, MRS. CLARK comes to the door of the store and calls him.)

MRS. CLARK.

(Drawlingly) Columbus!

LUM.

(Wearily) Ma'am?

MRS. CLARK.

De Mayor say for you to go round in de back yard and tie up old lady Jackson's mule what's trampin' aup all de tomatoes in my garden.

LUM.

All right. (Leaving card game.) Wait till I come back, folkses.

LIGE.

Oh, hum! (Yawning and putting down the deck of cards) Lum's sho a busy marshall. Say, ain't Dave and Jim been round here yet? I feel kinder like hearin' a little music 'bout now.

BOY.

Naw, they ain't been here today. You-all know they ain't so thick nohow as they was since Daisy Bailey come back and they started runnin' after her.

WOMAN.

You mean since she started runnin' after them, the young hussy.

MRS. CLARK.

(In doorway) She don't mean 'em no good.

WALTER.

That's a shame, ain't it now? (Enter LUM from around back of store. He jumps on the porch and takes his place at the card box.)

LUM.

(To the waiting players) All right, boys! Turn it on and let the bad luck happen.

LIGE.

My deal. (He begins shuffling the cards with an elaborate fan-shape movement.)

VOICE AT TABLE.

Look out there, Lige, you shuffling mighty lot. Don't carry the cub to us.

LIGE.

Aw, we ain't gonna cheat you ... we gonna beat you. (He slams down the cards for LUM BOGER to cut.) Wanta cut 'em?

LUM.

No, ain't no need of cutting a rabbit out when you can twist him out. Deal 'em. (LIGE deals out the cards.)

CLARK'S VOICE.

(Inside the store) You, Mattie! (MRS. CLARK, who has been standing in the door, quickly turns and goes inside.)

LIGE.

Y-e-e-e! Spades! (The game is started.)

LUM.

Didn't snatch that jack, did you?

LIGE.

Aw, no, ain't snatched no jack. Play.

WALTER.

(LUM'S partner) Well, here it is, partner. What you want me to play for you?

LUM.

Play jus' like I'm in New York, partner. But we gotta try to catch that jack.

LIGE.

(Threateningly) Stick out your hand and draw back a nub.

(WALTER THOMAS plays.)

WALTER.

I'm playin' a diamond for you, partner.

LUM.

I done tole you you ain't got no partner.

LIGE.

Heh, Heh! Partner, we got 'em. Pull off wid your king. Dey got to play 'em. (When that trick is turned, triumphantly:) Didn't I tell you, partner? (Stands on his feet and slams down with his ace violently) Now, come up under this ace. Aw, hah, look at ol' low, partner. I knew I was gonna catch 'em. (When LUM plays) Ho, ho, there goes the queen.... Now, the jack's a gentleman.... Now, I'm playin' my knots. (Everybody plays and the hand is ended.) Partner, high, low, jack and the game and four.

WALTER.

Give me them cards. I believe you-all done give me the cub that time. Look at me … this is Booker T Washington dealing these cards. (Shuffles cards grandly and gives them to LIGE to cut.) Wanta cut 'em?

LIGE.

Yeah, cut 'em and shoot 'em. I'd cut behind my ma. (He cuts the cards.)

WALTER.

(Turning to player at left, FRANK, LIGE'S partner) What you saying, Frank?

FRANK.

I'm beggin'. (LIGE is trying to peep at cards.)

WALTER.

(Turning to LIGE) Stop peepin' at them cards, Lige. (To FRANK) Did you say you was beggin' or standin'?

FRANK.

I'm beggin'.

WALTER.

Get up off your knees. Go ahead and tell 'em I sent you.

FRANK.

Well, that makes us four.

WALTER.

I don't care if you is. (Pulls a quarter out of his pocket and lays it down on the box.) Twenty-five cents says I know the best one. Let's go. (Everybody puts down a quarter.)

FRANK.

What you want me to play for you partner?

LIGE.

Play me a club. (The play goes around to dealer, WALTER, who gets up and takes the card off the top of the deck and slams it down on the table.)

WALTER.

Get up ol' deuce of deamonds and gallop off with your load. (TO LUM) Partner, how many times you seen the deck?

LUM.

Two times.

WALTER.

Well, then I'm gonna pull off, partner. Watch this ol' queen. (Everyone plays) Ha! Ha! Wash day and no soap. (Takes the jack of diamonds and sticks him up on his forehead. Stands up on his feet.) Partner, I'm dumping to you … play your king. (When it comes to his play LUM, too, stands up. The others get up and they, too, excitedly slam their cards down.) Now, come on in this kitchen and let me splice that cabbage! (He slams down the ace of diamonds. Pats the jack on his forehead, sings:) Hey, hey, back up, jenny, get your load. (Talking) Dump to that jack, boys, dump to it. High, low, jack and the game and four. One to go. We're four wid you, boys.

LIGE.

Yeah, but you-all playin' catch-up.

FRANK.

Gimme them cards … lemme deal some.

LIGE.

Frank, now you really got responsibility on you. They's got one game on us.

FRANK.

Aw, man, I'm gonna deal 'em up a mess. This deal's in the White House. (He shuffles and puts the cards down for WALTER to cut.) Cut 'em.

WALTER.

Nope, I never cut green timber. (FRANK deals and turns the card up.)

FRANK.

Hearts, boys. (He turns up an ace.)

LUM.

Aw, you snatched that ace, nigger.

WALTER.

Yeah, they done carried the cub to us, partner.

LIGE.

Oh, he didn't do no such a thing. That ace was turned fair. We jus' too hard for you … we eats our dinner out a the blacksmith shop.

WALTER.

Aw, you all cheatin'. You know it wasn't fair.

FRANK.

Aw, shut up, you all jus' whoopin' and hollerin' for nothin'. Tryin' to bully the game. (FRANK and LIGE rise and shake hands grandly.)

LIGE.

Mr. Hoover, you sho is a noble president. We done stuck these niggers full of cobs. They done got scared to play us.

LIGE (?) Scared to play you? Get back down to this table, let me spread my mess.

LOUNGER.

Yonder comes Elder Simms. You all better squat that rabbit. They'll be having you all up in the church for playin' cards.

(FRANK grabs up the cards and puts them in his pocket quickly. Everybody picks up the money and looks unconcerned as the preacher enters. Enter ELDER SIMMS with his two prim-looking little children by the hand.)

ELDER SIMMS.

How do, children. Right warm for this time in November, ain't it?

VOICE.

Yes sir, Reverend, sho is. How's Sister Simms?

SIMMS.

She's feelin' kinda po'ly today. (Goes on in store with his children)

VOICE.

(Whispering loudly) Don't see how that great big ole powerful woman could be sick. Look like she could go bear huntin' with her fist.

ANOTHER VOICE.

She look jus' as good as you-all's Baptist pastor's wife. Pshaw, you ain't seen no big woman, nohow, man. I seen one once so big she went to whip her little boy and he run up under her belly and hid six months 'fore she could find him.

ANOTHER VOICE.

Well, I knowed a woman so little that she had to get up on a soap box to look over a grain of sand.

(REV. SIMMS comes out of store, each child behind him sucking a stick of candy.)

SIMMS.

(To his children) Run on home to your mother and don't get dirty on the way. (The two children start primly off down the street but just out of sight one of them utters a loud cry.)

SIMMS'S CHILD.

(Off stage) Papa, papa. Nunkie's trying to lick my candy.

SIMMS.

I told you to go on and leave them other children alone.

VOICE ON PORCH.

(Kidding) Lum, whyn't you tend to your business.

(TOWN MARSHALL rises and shoos the children off again.)

LUM.

You all varmints leave them nice chillun alone.

LIGE.

(Continuing the lying on porch) Well, you all done seen so much, but I bet you ain't never seen a snake as big as the one I saw when I was a boy up in middle Georgia. He was so big couldn't hardly move his self. He laid in one spot so long he growed moss on him and everybody thought he was a log, till one day I set down on him and went to sleep, and when I woke up that snake done crawled to Florida. (Loud laughter.)

FRANK.

(Seriously) Layin' all jokes aside though now, you all remember that rattlesnake I killed last year was almost as big as that Georgia snake.

VOICE.

How big, you say it was, Frank?

FRANK.

Maybe not quite as big as that, but jus' about fourteen feet.

VOICE.

(Derisively) Gimme that lyin' snake. That snake wasn't but four foot long when you killed him last year and you done growed him ten feet in a year.

ANOTHER VOICE.

Well, I don't know about that. Some of the snakes around here is powerful long. I went out in my front yard yesterday right after the rain and killed a great big ol' cottonmouth.

SIMMS.

This sho is a snake town. I certainly can't raise no chickens for 'em. They kill my little biddies jus' as fast as they hatch out. And yes ... if I hadn't cut them weeds out of the street in front of my parsonage, me or some of my folks woulda been snake-bit right at our front door. (To whole crowd) Whyn't you all cut down these weeds and clean up these streets?

HAMBO.

Well, the Mayor ain't said nothin' 'bout it.

SIMMS.

When the folks misbehaves in this town I think they oughta lock 'em up in a jail and make 'em work their fine out on the streets, then these weeds would be cut down.

VOICE.

How we gonna do that when we ain't got no jail?

SIMMS.

Well, you sho needs a jail ... you-all needs a whole lot of improvements round this town. I ain't never pastored no town so way-back as this one here.

CLARK.

(Who has lately emerged from the store, fanning himself, overhears this last remark and bristles up) What's that you say 'bout this town?

SIMMS.

I say we needs some improvements here in this town ... that's what.

CLARK.

(In a powerful voice) And what improvements you figgers we needs?

SIMMS.

A whole heap. Now, for one thing we really does need a jail, Mayor. We oughta stop runnin' these people out of town that misbehaves, and lock 'em up. Others towns has jails, everytown I ever pastored had a jail. Don't see how come we can't have one.

CLARK.

(Towering angrily above the preacher) Now, wait a minute, Simms. Don't you reckon the man who knows how to start a town knows how to run it? I paid two hundred dollars out of this right hand for this land and walked out here and started this town befo' you was born. I ain't like some of you new niggers, come here when grapes' ripe. I was here to cut new ground, and I been Mayor ever since.

SIMMS.

Well, there ain't no sense in no one man stayin' Mayor all the time.

CLARK.

Well, it's my town and I can be mayor jus' as long as I want to. It was me that put this town on the map.

SIMMS.

What map you put it on, Joe Clark? I ain't seen it on no map.

CLARK.

(Indignant) I God! Listen here, Elder Simms. If you don't like the way I run this town, just' take your flat feets right on out and git yonder crost the woods. You ain't been here long enough to say nothin' nohow.

HAMBO.

(From a nail keg) Yeah, you Methodist niggers always telling people how to run things.

TAYLOR.

(Practically unheard by the others) We do so know how to run things, don't we? Ain't Brother Mayor a Methodist, and ain't the school-teacher a ...? (His remarks are drowned out by the others.)

SIMMS.

No, we don't like the way you're runnin' things. Now looka here, (Pointing at the Marshall) You got that lazy Lum Boger here

39

for marshall and he ain't old enough to be dry behind his ears yet ... and all these able-bodied means in this town! You won't 'low nobody else to run a store 'ceptin' you. And looka yonder (happening to notice the street light) only street lamp in town, you got in front of your place. (Indignantly) We pay the taxes and you got the lamp.

VILLAGER.

Don't you-all fuss now. How come you two always yam-yamming at each other?

CLARK.

How come this fly-by-night Methodist preacher over here ... ain't been here three months ... tries to stand up on my store porch and tries to tell me how to run my town? (MATTIE CLARK, the Mayor's wife, comes timidly to the door, wiping her hands on her apron.) Ain't no man gonna tell me how to run my town. I God, I 'lected myself in and I'm gonna run it. (Turns and sees wife standing in door. Commandingly.) I God, Mattie, git on back in there and wait on that store!

MATTIE.

(Timidly) Jody, somebody else wantin' stamps.

CLARK.

I God, woman, what good is you? Gwan, git in. Look like between women and preachers a man can't have no peace. (Exit CLARK.)

SIMMS.

(Continuing his argument) Now, when I pastored in Jacksonville you oughta see what kinda jails they got there....

LOUNGER.

White folks needs jails. We colored folks don't need no jail.

ANOTHER VILLAGER.

Yes, we do, too. Elder Simms is right….

(The argument becomes a hubbub of voices.)

TAYLOR.

(Putting down his basket) Now, I tell you a jail….

MRS. TAYLOR.

(Emerging from the store door, arms full of groceries, looking at her husband) Yeah, and if you don't shut up and git these rations home I'm gonna be worse on you than a jail and six judges. Pickup that basket and let's go. (TONY meekly picks up the basket and he and his wife exit as the sound of an approaching guitar is heard off stage.)

(Two carelessly dressed, happy-go-lucky fellows enter together. One is fingering a guitar without playing any particular tune, and the other has his hat cocked over his eyes in a burlesque, dude-like manner. There are casual greetings.)

WALTER.

Hey, there, bums, how's tricks?

LIGE.

What yo' sayin', boys?

HAMBO.

Good evenin' sons.

LIGE.

How did you-all make out this evenin', boys?

JIM.

Oh, them white folks at the party shelled out right well. Kept Dave busy pickin' it up. How much did we make today, Dave?

DAVE.

(Striking his pocket) I don't know, boy, but feels right heavy here. Kept me pickin' up money just like this…. (As JIM picks a few dance chords, Dave gives a dance imitation of how he picked up the coins from the ground as the white folks threw them.) We count it after while. Woulda divided up with you already if you hadn't left me when you seen Daisy comin' by. Let's sit down on the porch and rest now.

LIGE.

She sho is lookin' stylish and pretty since she come back with her white folks from up North. Wearin' the swellest clothes. And that coal-black hair of hers jus' won't quit.

MATTIE CLARK.

(In doorway) I don't see what the mens always hanging after Daisy Taylor for.

CLARK.

(Turning around on the porch) I God, you back here again. Who's tendin' that store? (MATTIE disappears inside.)

DAVE.

Well, she always did look like new money to me when she was here before.

JIM.

Well, that's all you ever did get was a look.

DAVE.

That's all you know! I bet I get more than that now.

JIM.

You might git it but I'm the man to use it. I'm a bottom fish.

DAVE.

Aw, man. You musta been walking round here fast asleep when Daisy was in this county last. You ain't seen de go I had with her.

JIM.

No, I ain't seen it. Bet you didn't have no letter from her while she been away.

DAVE.

Bet you didn't neither.

JIM.

Well, it's just cause she can't write. If she knew how to scratch with a pencil I'd had a ton of 'em.

DAVE.

Shaw, man! I'd had a post office full of 'em.

OLD WOMAN.

You-all ought to be shame, carrying on over a brazen heifer like Daisy Taylor. Jus' cause she's been up North and come back, I reckon you cutting de fool sho 'nough now. She ain't studying none of you-all nohow. All she wants is what you got in your pocket.

JIM.

I likes her but she won't git nothin' outa me. She never did. I wouldn't give a poor consumpted cripple crab a crutch to cross the River Jurdon.

DAVE.

I know I ain't gonna give no woman nothin'. I wouldn't give a dog a doughnut if he treed a terrapin.

LIGE.

Youse a cottontail dispute ... both of you. You'd give her anything you got. You'd give her Georgia with a fence 'round it.

OLD MAN.

Yeah, and she'd take it, too.

LINDSAY.

Don't discriminate the woman like that. That ain't nothing but hogism. Ain't nothin' the matter with Daisy, she's all right.

(Enter TEETS and BOOTSIE tittering coyly and switching themselves.)

BOOTSIE.

Is you seen my mama?

OLD WOMAN.

You know you ain't lookin' for no mama. Jus' come back down here to show your shape and fan around awhile. (BOOTSIE and TEETS going into the store.)

BOOTSIE & TEETS.

No, we ain't. We'se come to get our mail.

OLD WOMAN.

(After girls enter store) Why don't you all keep up some attention to these nice girls here, Bootsie and Teets. They wants to marry.

DAVE.

Aw, who thinkin' 'bout marryin' now? They better stay home and eat their own pa's rations. I gotta buy myself some shoes.

JIM.

The woman I'm gonna marry ain't born yet and her maw is dead.

(GIRLS come out giggling and exit.) (JIM begins to strum his guitar lightly at first as the talk goes on.)

CLARK.

(To DAVE and JIM) Two of the finest gals that ever lived and friendly jus' like you-all is. You two boys better take 'em back and stop them shiftless ways.

HAMBO.

Yeah, hurry up and do somethin'! I wants to taste a piece yo' weddin' cake.

JIM.

(Embarrassed but trying to be jocular) Whut you trying to rush me up so fast?... Look at Will Cody here (Pointing to little man on porch) he been promising to bring his already wife down for two months ... and nair one of us ain't seen her yet.

DAVE.

Yeah, how you speck me to haul in a brand new wife when he can't lead a wagon-broke wife eighteen miles? Me, I'm going git one soon's Cody show me his'n. (General sly laughter at CODY'S expense.)

WALTER.

(Snaps his fingers and pretends to remember something) Thass right, Cody. I been intending to tell you.... I know where you kin buy a ready-built house for you and yo' wife. (Calls into the store.) Hey, Clark, cime on out here and tell Cody 'bout dat Bradley house. (To CODY.) I know you wants to git a place of yo' own so you kin settle down.

HAMBO.

He done moved so much since he been here till every time he walk out in his back yeard his chickens lay down and cross they legs.

LINDSAY.

Cody, I thought you tole us you was going up to Sanford to bring dat 'oman down here last Sat'day.

LIGE.

That ain't de way he tole me 'bout it. Look, fellers, (Getting up and putting one hand on his hips and one finger of the other hand against his chin coquettishly) Where you reckon I'll be next Sat'day night?… Sittin' up side of Miz Cody. (Great burst of laughter.)

SYKES JONES.

(Laughing) Know what de folks tole me in Sanford? Dat was another man's wife. (Guffaws.)

CODY.

(Feebly) Aw, you don't know whut you talkin' bout.

JONES.

Naw, I don't know, but de folks in Sanford does. (Laughing) Dey tell me when dat lady's husband come home Sat'day night, ole Cody jumped out de window. De man grabbed his old repeater and run out in de yard to head him off. When Cody seen him come round de corner de house (Gesture) he flopped his wings and flew up on de fence. De man thowed dat shotgun dead on him. (Laughs) Den, man! Cody flopped his wings lak a buzzard (Gesture) and sailed on off. De man dropped to his knees lak dis (Gesture of kneeling on one knee and taking aim) Die! die! die! (Supposedly sound of shots as the gun is moved in a circle following the course of Cody's supposed flight) Cody just flew right on off and lit on a hill two miles off. Then, man! (Gesture of swift flight) In ten minutes he was back here in Eatonville and in he bed.

WALTER.

I passed there and seen his house shakin', but I didn't know how come.

HAMBO.

Aw, leave de boy alone…. If you don't look out some of y'all going to have to break his record.

LIGE.

I'm prepared to break it now. (General laughter.)

JIM.

Well, anyhow, I don't want to marry and leave Dave … yet awhile. (Picking a chord.)

DAVE.

And I ain't gonna leave Jim. We been palling around together ever since we hollered titty mama, ain't we, boy?

JIM.

Sho is. (Music of the guitar increases in volume. DAVE shuffles a few steps and the two begin to sing.)

JIM: Rabbit on the log.

I ain't got no dog.

How am I gonna git him?

God knows.

DAVE:

Rabbit on the log.

Ain't got no dog.

Shoot him with my rifle

Bam! Bam!

(Some of the villagers join in song and others get up and march around the porch in time with the music. BOOTSIE and TEETS re-enter, TEETS sticking her letter down the neck of her blouse. JOE LINDSAY grabs TEETS and WALTER THOMAS grabs BOOTSIE. There is dancing, treating and general jollification. Little children dance the parse-me-la. The music fills the air just as the sun begins to go down. Enter DAISY TAYLOR coming down the road toward the store.)

CLARK.

(Bawls out from the store porch) I God, there's Daisy again.

(Most of the dancing stops, the music slows down and then stops completely. DAVE and JIM greet DAISY casually as she approaches the porch.)

JIM.

Well, Daisy, we knows you, too.

DAVE.

Gal, youse jus' as pretty as a speckled pup.

DAISY.

(Giggling) I see you two boys always playin' and singin' together. That music sounded right good floating down the road.

JIM.

Yeah, child, we'se been playin'for the white folks all week. We'se playin'for the colored now.

DAVE.

(Showing off, twirling his dancing feet) Yeah, we're standin'on our abstract and livin'on our income.

OLD MAN.

Um-ump, but they ain't never workin'. Just round here playing as usual.

JIM.

Some folks think you ain't workin'lessen you smellin'a mule. (He sits back down on box and picks at his guitar.) Think you gotta be beatin'a man to his barn every mornin'.

VOICE.

Glad to be round home with we-all again, ain't you Daisy?

DAISY.

Is I glad? I jus' got off special early this evenin'to come over here and see everybody. I was kinda 'fraid sundown would catch me 'fore I got round that lake. Don't know how I'm gonna walk back to my workin'place in the dark by muself.

DAVE.

Don't no girl as good-lookin'as you is have to go home by herself tonight.

JIM.

No, cause I'm here.

DAVE.

(To DAISY) Don't you trust yourself round that like wid all them 'gators and moccasins with that nigger there, Daisy (Pointing at JIM) He's jus' full of rabbit blood. What you need is a real man … with good feet. (Cutting a dance step.)

DAISY.

I ain't thinking 'bout goin'home yet. I'm goin'in the store.

JIM.

What you want in the store?

DAISY.

I want some gum.

DAVE.

(Starting toward door) Girl, you don't have to go in there to git no gum. I'll go in there and buy you a carload of gum. What kind you want?

DAISY.

Bubble gum. (DAVE goes in the store with his hand in his pocket. The sun is setting and the twilight deepens.)

JIM.

(Pulling package out of his pocket and laughing) Here your gum, baby. What it takes to please the ladies, I totes it. I don't have to go get it, like Dave. What you gimme for it?

DAISY.

A bushel and a peck, and a hug around the neck. (She embraces JIM playfully. He hands her the gum, patting his shoulder as he sits on box.) Oh, thank you. Youse a ready man.

JIM.

Yeah, there's a lot of good parts to me. You can have West Tampa if you want it.

DAISY.

You always was a nice quiet boy, Jim.

DAVE.

(Emerging from the store with a package of gum) Here's your gum, Daisy.

JIM.

Oh, youse late. She's done got gum now. Chaw that yourself.

DAVE.

(Slightly peeved and surprised) Hunh, you mighty fast here now with Daisy but you wasn't that fast gettin'out of that white man's chicken house last week.

JIM.

Who you talkin"bout?

DAVE.

Hoo-oo? (Facetiously) You ain't no owl. Your feet don't fit no limb.

JIM.

Aw, nigger, hush.

DAVE.

Aw, hush, yourself. (He walks away for a minute as DAISY turns to meet some newcomers. DAVE throws his package of gum down on the ground. It breaks and several children scramble for the pieces. An old man, very drunk, carrying an empty jug enters on left and staggers tipsily across stage.) (MAYOR JOE CLARK emerges from the store and looks about for his marshall.)

CLARK.

(Bellowing) Lum Boger!

LUM BOGER.

(Eating a stalk of cane) Yessir!

CLARK.

I God, Lum, take your lazy self off that keg and go light that town lamp. All summer long you eatin' up my melon, and all winter long you chawin' up my cane. What you think this town is payin' you for? Laying round here doin' nothin'? Can't you see it's gettin' dark?

(LUM BOGER rises lazily and takes the soap box down stage, stands on it to light the lamp, discovers no oil in it and goes in store. In a few moments he comes out of store, fills the lamp and lights it.)

DAISY.

(Coming back toward JIM) Ain't you all gonna play and sing a little somethin' for me? I ain't heard your all's music much for so long.

JIM.

Play anything you want, Daisy. Don't make no difference what 'tis I can pick it. Where's that old coon, Dave? (Looking around for his partner.)

LIGE.

(Calling Dave, who is leaning against post at opposite end of porch) Come here, an' get warmed up for Daisy.

DAVE.

Aw, ma throat's tired.

JIM.

Leave the baby be.

DAISY.

Come on, sing a little, Dave.

DAVE.

(Going back toward Jim) Well, seeing who's asking … all right. What song yo like, Daisy?

DAISY.

Um-m. Lemme think.

VOICE ON PORCH.

"Got on the train, didn't have no fare".

DAISY.

(Gaily) Yes, that one. That's a good one.

JIM.

(Begins to tune up. DAVE touches Daisy's hand.)

VOICE.

(In fun) Hunh, you all wouldn't play at the hall last week when we asked you.

VOICE OF SPITEFUL OLD WOMAN.

Daisy wasn't here then.

ANOTHER VOICE.

(Teasingly) All you got to do to some men is to shake a skirt tail in their face and they goes off their head.

DAVE.

(To JIM who is still tuning up) Come if you're comin'boy, let's go if you gwine. (The full melody of the guitar comes out in a lively, old-fashioned tune.)

VOICE.

All right now, boys, do it for Daisy jus' as good as you do for dem white folks over in Maitland.

DAVE & JIM.

(Beginning to sing)

Got on the train,

Didn't have no fare,

But I rode some,

I rode some.

Got on the train,

Didn't have no fare,

But I rode some,

But I rode some.

Got on the train,

Didn't have no fare,

Conductor asked me what I'm doin'there,

But I rode some!

Grabbed me by the neck

And led me to the door.

But I rode some,

But I rode some.

Grabbed me by the neck

And led me to the door.

But I rode some,

But I rode some.

Grabbed me by the neck,

And led me to the door.

Rapped me cross the head with a forty-four,

But I rode some.

First thing I saw in jail

Was a pot of peas.

But I rode some,

But I rode some.

First thing I saw in jail

Was a pot of peas.

But I rode some,

But I rode some.

The peas was good,

The meat was fat,

Fell in love with the chain gang jus' for that,

But I rode some.

(DAVE acts out the song in dancing pantomime and when it ends there are shouts and general exclamations of approval from the crowd.)

VOICES.

I don't blame them white folks for goin' crazy 'bout that....

OLD MAN.

Oh, when I was a young boy I used to swing the gals round on that piece.

DAISY.

(TO JIM) Seem like your playin' gits better and better.

DAVE.

(Quickly) And how 'bout my singin'? (Everybody laughs.)

VOICES IN THE CROWD.

Ha! Ha! Ol' Dave's gittin' jealous when she speaks o' Jim.

JIM.

(To DAVE, in fun) Ain't nothin' to it but my playin'. You ain't got no singin' voice. If that's singin', God's a gopher.

DAVE.

(Half-seriously) My singin' is a whole lot better'n your playin'. You jus' go along and fram. The reason why the white folks gives us money is cause I'm singin'.

JIM.

Yeah?

DAVE.

And you can't dance.

VOICE IN THE CROWD.

You oughta dance. Big as your feet is, Dave.

DAISY.

(Diplomatically) Both of you all is wonderful and I would like to see Dave dance a little.

DAVE.

There now, I told you. What did I tell you. (To JIM) Stop woofing and pick a little tune there so that I can show Daisy somethin'.

JIM.

Pick a tune? I bet if you fool with me I'll pick your bones jus' like a buzzard did the rabbit. You can't sing and now you wants to dance.

DAVE.

Yeah, and I'll lam your head. Come on and play, good-for-nothing.

JIM.

All right, then. You say you can dance ... show these people what you can do. But don't bring that little stuff I been seein'you doin' all these years. (JIM plays and DAVE dances, various members of the crowd keep time with their hands and feet, DAISY looks on enjoying herself immensely.)

DAISY.

(As DAVE cuts a very fancy step) I ain't seen nothin'like this up North. Dave you sho hot.

(As DAVE cuts a more complicated step the crowd applauds, but just as the show begins to get good, suddenly JIM stops playing.)

DAVE.

(Surprised) What's the matter, buddy?

JIM.

(Envious of the attention DAVE has been getting from DAISY, disgustedly) Oh, nigger, I'm tired of seein'you cut the fool. 'Sides that, I been playin'all afternoon for the white folks.

DAISY.

But I though you was playin' for me now, Jim.

JIM.

Yeah, I'd play all night long for you, but I'm gettin' sick of Dave round here showin' off. Let him git somethin' and play for himself if he can. (An OLD MAN with a lighted lantern enters.)

DAISY.

(Coyly) Well, honey, play some more for me, then, and don't mind Dave. I reckon he done danced enough. Play me "Shake That Thing".

OLD MAN WITH LANTERN.

Sho, you ain't stopped, is you, boy? Music sound mighty good floatin' down that dark road.

OLD WOMAN.

Yeah, Jim, go on play a little more. Don't get to acting so niggerish this evening.

DAVE.

Aw, let the ol' darky alone. Nobody don't want to hear him play, nohow. I know I don't.

JIM.

Well, I'm gonna play. (And he begins to pick "Shake That Thing". TEETS and BOOTSIE begin to dance with LIGE MOSELY and FRANK WARRICK. As the tune gets good, DAVE cannot resist the music either.)

DAVE.

Old nigger's eevil but he sho can play. (He begins to do a few steps by himself, then twirls around in front of DAISY and approaches her. DAISY, overcome by the music, begins to step rhythmically toward DAVE and together they dance unobserved by JIM, absorbed in picking his guitar.)

DAISY.

Look here, baby, at this new step I learned up North.

DAVE.

You can show me anything, sugar lump.

DAISY.

Hold me tight now. (But just as they begin the new movement JIM notices DAISY and DAVE. He stops playing again and lays his guitar down.)

VOICES IN THE CROWD.

(Disgustedly) Aw, come on, Jim…. You must be jealous….

JIM.

No, I ain't jealous. I jus' get tired of seein'that ol' nigger clownin'all the time.

DAVE.

(Laughing and pointing to JIM on porch) Look at that mad baby. Take that lip up off the ground. Got your mouth stuck out jus' because some one is enjoying themselves. (He comes up and pushes JIM playfully.)

JIM.

You better go head and let me alone. (TO DAISY) Come here, Daisy!

LIGE.

That's just what I say. Niggers can't have no fun without someone getting mad … specially over a woman.

JIM.

I ain't mad…. Daisy, 'scuse me, honey, but that fool, Dave….

DAVE.

I ain't mad neither…. Jim always tryin'to throw off on me. But you can't joke him.

DAISY.

(Soothingly) Aw, now, now!

JIM.

You ain't jokin'. You means that, nigger. And if you tryin'to get hot, first thing, you can pull of my blue shirt you put on this morning.

DAVE.

Youse a got that wrong. I ain't got on no shirt of yours.

JIM.

Yes, you is got on my shirt, too. Don't tell me you ain't got on my shirt.

DAVE.

Well, even if I is, you can just lift your big plantations out of my shoes. You can just foot it home barefooted.

JIM.

You try to take any shoes offa me!

LIGE.

(Pacifying them) Aw, there ain't no use of all that. What you all want to start this quarreling for over a little jokin'.

JIM.

Nobody's quarreling…. I'm just playin'a little for Daisy and Dave's out there clownin'with her.

CLARK.

(In doorway) I ain't gonna have no fussin'round my store, no way. Shut up, you all.

JIM.

Well, Mayor Clark, I ain't mad with him. We'se been friends all our lives. He's slept in my bed and wore my clothes and et my grub….

DAVE.

I et your grub? And many time as you done laid down with your belly full of my grandma's collard greens. You done et my meat and bread a whole lot more times than I et your stewed fish-heads.

JIM.

I'd rather eat stewed fish-heads than steal out of other folkses houses so much till you went to sleep on the roost and fell down one night and broke up the settin'hen. (Loud laughter from the crowd)

DAVE.

Youse a liar if you say I stole anybody's chickens. I didn't have to. But you … 'fore you started goin'around with me, playin' that little box of yours, you was so hungry you had the white mouth. If it wasn't for these white folks throwin'*me* money for *my* dancin', you would be thin as a whisper right now.

JIM.

(Laughing sarcastically) Your dancin'! You been leapin'around here like a tailless monkey in a wash pot for a long time and nobody was payin' no 'tention to you, till I come along playing.

LINDSAY.

Boys, boys, that ain't no way for friends to carry on.

DAISY.

Well, if you all gonna keep up this quarrelin' and carryin' on I'm goin' home. 'Bout time for me to be gittin' back to my white folks anyhow. It's dark now. I'm goin', even if I have to go by myself. I shouldn't a stopped by here nohow.

JIM.

(Stopping his quarrel) You ain't gonna go home by yourself. I'm goin' with you.

DAVE.

(Singing softly)

It may be so,

I don't know.

But it sounds to me

Like a lie.

WALTER.

Dave ain't got as much rabbit blood as folks thought.

DAVE.

Tell 'em 'bout me. (Turns to DAISY) Won't you choose a treat on me, Miss Daisy, 'fore we go?

DAISY.

(Coyly) Yessir, thank you. I wants a drink of soda water.

(DAVE pulls his hat down over his eyes, whirls around and offers his arm to DAISY. They strut into the store, DAVE gazing contemptuously at JIM as he passes. Crowd roars with laughter, much to the embarrassment of JIM.)

LIGE.

Ol' fast Dave jus' runnin'the hog right over you, Jim.

WALTER.

Thought you was such a hot man.

LUM BOGER.

Want me to go in there and put Daisy under arrest and bring her to you?

JIM.

(Sitting down on the edge of porch with one foot on the step and lights a cigarette pretending not to be bothered.) Aw, I'll get her when I want her. Let him treat her, but see who struts around that lake and down the railroad with her by and by.

(DAVE and DAISY emerge from the store, each holding a bottle of red soda pop and laughing together. As they start down the steps DAVE accidentally steps on JIM's outstretched foot. JIM jumps up and pushes DAVE back, causing him to spill the red soda all over his white shirt front.)

JIM.

Stay off my foot, you big ox.

DAVE.

Well, you don't have to wet me all up, do you, and me in company? Why don't you put your damn foot in your pocket?

DAISY.

(Wiping DAVE'S shirt front with her handkerchief) Aw, ain't that too bad.

JIM.

(To DAVE) Well, who's shirt did I wet? It's mine, anyhow, ain't it?

DAVE.

(Belligerently) Well, if it's your shirt, then you come take it off me. I'm tired of your lip.

JIM.

Well, I will.

DAVE.

Well, put your fist where you lip is. (Pushing DAISY aside.)

DAISY.

(Frightened) I want to go home. Now, don't you all boys fight.

(JIM attempts to come up the steps. DAVE pushes him back and he stumbles and falls in the dust. General excitement as the crowd senses a fight.)

LITTLE BOY.

(On the edge of crowd) Fight, fight, you're no kin. Kill one another, won't be no sin. Fight, fight, you're no kin.

(JIM jumps up and rushes for DAVE as the latter starts down the steps. DAVE meets him with his fist squarely in the face and causes him to step backward, confused.)

DAISY.

(Still on porch, half crying) Aw, my Lawd! I want to go home.

(General hubbub, women's cries of "Don't let 'em fight." "Why don't somebody stop 'em?" "What kind of men is you all, sit there and let them boys fight like that." Men's voices urging the fight: "Aw, let 'em fight." "Go for him, Dave." "Slug him, Jim."

JIM makes another rush toward the steps. He staggers DAVE. DAVE knocks JIM sprawling once more. This time JIM grabs the mule bone as he rises, rushes DAVE, strikes DAVE over the head with it and knocks him out. DAVE falls prone on his back. There is great excitement.)

OLD WOMAN.

(Screams) Lawdy, is he kilt? (Several men rush to the fallen man.)

VOICE.

Run down to the pump and get a dipper o' water.

CLARK.

(To his wife in door) Mattie, come out of that store with a bottle of witch hazely oil quick as you can. Jim Weston, I'm gonna arrest you for this. You Lum Boger. Where is that marshall? Lum Boger! (LUM BOGER detaches himself from the crowd.) Arrest Jim.

LUM.

(Grabs JIM'S arm, relieves him of the mule bone and looks helplessly at the Mayor.) Now I got him arrested, what's I going to do with him?

CLARK.

Lock him up back yonder in my barn till Monday when we'll have the trial in de Baptist Church.

LINDSAY.

Yeah, just like all the rest of them Methodists … always tryin'to take undercurrents on people.

WALTER.

Ain't no worse then some of you Baptists, nohow. You all don't run this town. We got jus' as much to say as you have.

CLARK.

(Angrily to both men) Shut up! Done had enough arguing in front of my place. (To LUM BOGER) Take that boy on and lock him up in my barn. And save that mule bone for evidence.

(LUM BOGER leads JIM off toward the back of the store. A crowd follows him. Other men and women are busy applying restoratives to DAVE. DAISY stands alone, unnoticed in the center of the stage.)

DAISY.

(Worriedly) Now, who's gonna take me home?

::::: **CURTAIN**:::::

ACT TWO

SCENE I

SETTING: Village street scene; huge oak tree upstage center; a house or two on back drop. When curtain goes up, Sister LUCY TAYLOR is seen standing under the tree. She is painfully spelling it out.

(Enter SISTER THOMAS, a younger woman (In her thirties) at left.)

SISTER THOMAS.

Evenin', Sis Taylor.

SISTER TAYLOR.

Evenin'. (Returns to the notice)

SISTER THOMAS.

Whut you doin'? Readin'dat notice Joe Clark put up 'bout de meeting? (Approaches tree)

SISTER TAYLOR.

Is dat whut it says? I ain't much on readin'since I had my teeth pulled out. You know if you pull out dem eye teeth you ruins' yo' eye sight. (Turns back to notice) Whut it say?

SISTER THOMAS.

(Reading notice) "The trial of Jim Weston for assault and battery on Dave Carter wid a dangerous weapon will be held at Macedonia

Baptist Church on Monday, November 10, at three o'clock. All are welcome. By order of J. Clark, Mayor of Eatonville, Florida." (Turning to SISTER TAYLOR) Hit's makin' on to three now.

SISTER TAYLOR.

You mean it's right *now*. (Looks up at sun to tell time) Lemme go git ready to be at de trial 'cause I'm sho goin'to be there an' I ain't goin'to bite my tongue neither.

SISTER THOMAS.

I done went an' crapped a mess of collard greens for supper. I better go put 'em on 'cause Lawd knows when we goin'to git outa there an' my husband is one of them dat's gointer eat don't keer whut happen. I bet if judgment day was to happen tomorrow he'd speck I orter fix him a bucket to carry long. (She moves to exit, right)

SISTER TAYLOR.

All men favors they guts, chile. But what you think of all dis mess they got goin'on round here?

SISTER THOMAS.

I just think it's a sin an' a shame befo' de livin' justice de way dese Baptis' niggers is runnin'round here carryin'on.

SISTER TAYLOR.

Oh, they been puttin'out the brags ever since Sat'day night 'bout whut they gointer do to Jim. They thinks they runs this town. They tell me Rev. CHILDERS preached a sermon on it yistiddy.

SISTER THOMAS.

Lawd help us! He can't preach an' he look like 10 cents worth of have-mercy let lone gittin'up dere tryin'to throw slams at us. Now

all Elder Simms done wuz to explain to us our rights … whut you
think 'bout Joe Clarke runnin'round here takin'up for these ole
Baptist niggers?

SISTER TAYLOR.

De puzzle-gut rascal … we oughter have him up in conference an'
put him out de Methdis' faith. He don't b'long in there—wanter
tun dat boy outa town for nothin'.

SISTER THOMAS.

But we all know how come he so hot to law Jim outa town—hit's
to dig de foundation out from under Elder Simms.

SISTER TAYLOR.

Whut he wants do dat for?

SISTER THOMAS.

'Cause he wants to be a God-know-it-all an' a God-do-it-all an'
Simms is de onliest one in this town whut will buck up to him.

(Enter SISTER JONES, walking leisurely)

SISTER JONES.

Hello, Hoyt, hello, Lucy.

SISTER TAYLOR.

Goin'to de meetin'?

SISTER JONES.

Done got my clothes on de line an' I'm bound to be dere.

SISTER THOMAS.

Gointer testify for Jim?

SISTER JONES.

Naw, I reckon—don't make such difference to me which way de drop fall.… 'Tain't neither one of 'em much good.

SISTER TAYLOR.

I know it. I know it, Ida. But dat ain't de point. De crow we wants to pick is: Is we gointer set still an' let dese Baptist tell us when to plant an' when to pluck up?

SISTER JONES.

Dat is something to think about when you come to think 'bout it. (Starts to move on) Guess I better go ahead—see y'all later an tell you straighter.

(Enter ELDER SIMMS, right, walking fast, Bible under his arm, almost collides with SISTER JONES as she exits.)

SIMMS.

Oh, 'scuse me, Sister Jones. (She nods and smiles and exits.) How you do, Sister Taylor, Sister Thomas.

BOTH.

Good evenin', Elder.

SIMMS.

Sho is a hot day.

SISTER TAYLOR.

Yeah, de bear is walkin'de earth lak a natural man.

SISTER THOMAS.

Reverend, look like you headed de wrong way. It's almost time for de trial an' youse all de dependence we got.

SIMMS.

I know it. I'm tryin'to find de marshall so we kin go after Jim. I wants a chance to talk wid him a minute before court sets.

SISTER TAYLOR.

Y'think he'll come clear?

SIMMS.

(Proudly) I *know* it! (Shakes the Bible) I'm goin'to law 'em from Genesis to Revelation.

SISTER THOMAS.

Give it to 'em, Elder. Wear 'em out!

SIMMS.

We'se liable to havea new Mayor when all dis dust settle. Well, I better scuffle on down de road. (Exits, left.)

SISTER THOMAS.

Lord, lemme gwan home an' put dese greens on. (Looks off stage left) Here come Mayor Clark now, wid his belly settin'out in front of him like a cow catcher! His name oughter be Mayor Belly.

SISTER TAYLOR.

(Arms akimbo) Jus' look at him! Tryin'to look like a jigadier Breneral.

(Enter CLARK hot and perspiring. They look at him coldly.)

CLARK.

I God, de bear got me! (Silence for a moment) How y'all feelin', ladies?

SISTER TAYLOR.

Brother Mayor, I ain't one of these folks dat bite my tongue an' bust my gall—whut's inside got to come out! I can't see to my rest why you cloakin'in wid dese Baptist buzzards 'ginst yo' own church.

MAYOR CLARK.

I ain't cloakin'in wid *none*. I'm de Mayor of dis whole town I stands for de right an' ginst de wrong—I don't keer who it kill or cure.

SISTER THOMAS.

You think it's right to be runnin'dat boy off for nothin'?

CLARK.

I God! You call knockin'a man in de head wid a mule bone nothin'? 'Nother thin; I done missed nine of my best-layin'hens. I ain't sayin'Jim got 'em, but different people has tole me he burries a powerful lot of feathers in his back yard. I God, I'm a ruint man! (He starts towards the right exit, but LUM BOGER enters right.) I God, Lum, I been lookin'for you all day. It's almost three o'clock. (Hands him a key from his ring) Take dis key an' go fetch Jim Weston on to de church.

LUM.

Have you got yo' gavel from de lodge-room?

CLARK.

I God, that's right, Lum. I'll go get it from de lodge room whilst you go git de bone an' de prisoner. Hurry up! You walk like dead lice droppin'off you. (He exits right while LUM crosses stage towards left.)

SISTER TAYLOR.

Lum, Elder Simms been huntin'you—he's gone on down 'bout de barn. (She gestures)

LUM BOGER.

I reckon I'll overtake him. (Exit left.)

SISTER THOMAS.

I better go put dese greens on. My husband will kill me if he don't find no supper ready. Here come Mrs. Blunt. She oughter feel like a penny's worth of have-mercy wid all dis stink behind her daughter.

SISTER TAYLOR.

Chile, some folks don't keer. They don't raise they chillun; they drags 'em up. God knows if dat Daisy wuz mine, I'd throw her down an' put a hundred lashes on her back wid a plow-line. Here she come in de store Sat'day night (Acts coy and coquettish, burlesques DAISY'S walk) a wringing and a twisting! (Enter MRS. BLUNT, left.)

MRS. BLUNT.

How y'all sisters?

SISTER THOMAS.

Very well, Miz Blunt, how you?

MRS. BLUNT.

Oh, so-so.

MRS. TAYLOR.

I'm kickin', but not high.

MRS. BLUNT.

Well, thank God you still on prayin' ground an' in a Bible country. Me, I ain't so many today. De niggers got my Daisy's name all mixed up in dis mess.

MRS. TAYLOR.

You musn't mind dat, Sister Blunt. People jus' *will* talk. They's talkin' in New York an' they's talkin'in Georgy an' they's talkin' in Italy.

SISTER THOMAS.

Chile, if you talk folkses talk, they'll have you in de graveyard or in Chattahoochee one. You can't pay no 'tention to talk.

MRS. BLUNT.

Well, I know one thing. De man or women, chick or child, grizzly or gray, that tells me to my face anything wrong 'bout *my* chile, I'm goin' to take *my* fist (Rolls up right sleeve and gestures with right fist) and knock they teeth down they throat. (She looks ferocious) 'Case y'all know I raised my Daisy right round my feet till I let her go up north last year wid them white folks. I'd ruther her to be in de white folks' kitchen than walkin'de streets like some of dese girls round here. If I do say so, I done raised a lady. She can't help it if all dese mens get stuck on her.

MRS. TAYLOR.

You'se tellin' de truth, Sister Blunt. That's whut I always say: Don't confidence dese niggers. Do, they'll sho put you in de street.

MRS. THOMAS.

Naw indeed, never syndicate wid niggers. Do, they will distriminate you. They'll be an *anybody*. You goin'to de trial, ain't you?

MRS. BLUNT.

Just as sho as you snore. An' they better leave Daisy's name outa dis, too. I done told her and told her to come straight home from her work. Naw, she had to stop by dat store and skin her gums back wid dem trashy niggers. She better not leave them white folks today to come traipsin'over here scornin'her name all up wid dis nigger mess. Do, I'll kill her. No daughter of mine ain't goin'to do as she please, long as she live under de sound of my voice. (She crosses to right.)

MRS. THOMAS.

That's right, Sister Blunt. I glory in yo' spunk. Lord, I better go put on my supper.

(As MRS. BLUNT exits, right, REV. CHILDERS enters left with DAVE and DEACON LINDSAY and SISTER LEWIS. Very hostile glances from SISTERS THOMAS and TAYLOR toward the others.)

CHILDERS.

Good evenin', folks.

(SISTERS THOMAS and TAYLOR just grunt. MRS. THOMAS moves a step or two towards exit. Flirts her skirts and exits.)

LINDSAY.

(Angrily) Whut's de matter, y'all? Cat got yo' tongue?

MRS. TAYLOR.

More matter than you kin scatter all over Cincinnatti.

LINDSAY.

Go 'head on, Lucy Taylor. Go 'head on. You know a very little of yo' sugar sweetens my coffee. Go 'head on. Everytime you lift yo' arm you smell like a nest of yellow hammers.

MRS. TAYLOR.

Go 'head on yo'self. Yo' head look like it done wore out three bodies. Talkin" bout *me* smellin'—you smell lak a nest of grand daddies yo'self.

LINDSAY.

Aw rock on down de road, 'oman. Ah, don't wantuh change words wid yuh. Youse too ugly.

MRS. TAYLOR.

You ain't nobody's pretty baby, yo'self. You so ugly I betcha yo' wife have to spread uh sheet over yo' head tuh let sleep slip up on yuh.

LINDSAY.

(Threatening) You better git way from me while you able. I done tole you I don't wanter break a breath wid you. It's uh whole heap better tuh walk off on yo' own legs than it is to be toted off. I'm tired of yo' achin' round here. You fool wid me now an' I'll knock you into doll rags, Tony or no Tony.

MRS. TAYLOR.

(Jumping up in his face) Hit me? Hit me! I dare you tuh hit me. If you take dat dare, you'll steal uh hawg an' eat his hair.

LINDSAY.

Lemme gwan down to dat church befo' you make me stomp you. (He exits, right.)

MRS. TAYLOR.

You mean you'll *git* stomped. Ah'm goin' to de trial, too. De nex trial gointer be *me* for kickin' some uh you Baptist niggers around.

(A great noise is heard off stage left. The angry and jeering voices of children. MRS. TAYLOR looks off left and takes a step or two towards left exit as the noise comes nearer.)

VOICE OF ONE CHILD.

Tell her! Tell her! Turn her up and smell her. Yo' mama ain't got nothin' to do wid me.

MRS. TAYLOR.

(Hollering off left) You lil Baptis' haitians leave them chillun alone. If you don't, you better!

(Enter about ten children struggling and wrestling in a bunch. MRS. TAYLOR looks about on the ground for a stick to strike the children with.)

VOICE OF CHILD.

Hey! Hey! He's skeered tuh knock it off. Coward!

MRS. TAYLOR.

If y'all don't git on home!

SASSY LITTLE GIRL.

(Standing akimbo) I know you better not touch me, do my mama will 'tend to you.

MRS. TAYLOR.

(Making as if to strike her.) Shet up you nasty lil heifer, sassin' me! You ain't half raised.

(The little girl shakes herself at MRS. TAYLOR and is joined by two or three others.)

MRS. TAYLOR.

(Walkin' towards right exit.) I'm goin' on down to de church an' tell yo' mammy. But she ain't been half raised herself. (She exits right with several children making faces behind her.)

ONE BOY.

(To sassy GIRL) Aw, haw! Y'all ol' Baptis' ain't got no bookcase in yo' chuch. We went there one day an' I saw uh soda cracker box settin' up in de corner so I set down on it. (Pointing at sassy

GIRL) Know what ole Mary Ella say? (Jeering laughter) Willie, you git up off our library! Haw! Haw!

MARY ELLA.

Y'all ole Meth'dis' ain't got no window panes in yo' ole church.

ANOTHER GIRL.

(Takes center of stand, hands akimbo and shakes her hips) I don't keer whut y'all say, I'm a Meth'dis' bred an' uh Meth'dis' born an' when I'm dead there'll be uh Meth'dis' gone.

MARY ELLA.

(Snaps fingers under other girl's nose and starts singing.

Several join her.)

Oh Baptis', Baptis' is my name

My name's written on high

I got my lick in de Baptis' church

Gointer eat up de Meth'dis' pie.

(The Methodist children jeer and make faces. The Baptist camp make faces back; for a full minute there is silence while each camp tries to outdo the other in face making. The Baptist makes the last face.)

METHODIST BOY.

Come on, less us don't notice 'em. Less gwan down to de church an' hear de trial.

MARY ELLA.

Y'all ain't de onliest ones kin go. We goin', too.

WILLIE.

Aw, haw! Copy cats! (Makes face) Dat's right. Follow on behind us lak uh puppy dog tail. (They start walking toward right exit, switching their clothes behind.) Dat's right. Follow on behind us lak uh puppy dog tail. (They start walking toward right exit, switching their clothes behind.)

(Baptist children stage a rush and struggle to get in front of the Methodists. They finally succeed in flinging some of the Methodist children to the ground and some behind them and walk towards right exit haughtily switching their clothes.)

WILLIE.

(Whispers to his crowd) Less go round by Mosely's lot an' beat 'em there!

OTHERS.

All right!

WILLIE.

(Yellin' to Baptists) We wouldn't walk behind no ole Baptists!

(The Methodists turn and walk off towards left exit, switching their clothes as the Baptists are doing.)

SLOW CURTAIN

Angelina Weld Grimké

ACT THREE

SETTING: A high stretch of railroad track thru a luxurious Florida forest. It is near sundown.

ACTION: When the curtain rises there is no one on the stage, but there is a tremendous noise and hubbub off-stage right. There are yells of derision and shouts of anger. Part of the mob is trying to keep JIM in town, and part is driving him off. After a full minute of this, JIM enters with his guitar hanging around his neck and his coat over his shoulder. The sun is dropping low and red thru the forest. He is looking back angrily and shouting at the mob. A missile is thrown after him. JIM drops his coat and guitar and grabs up a piece of brick, and makes threatening gestures of throwing it.

JIM.

(Running back the way he came and hurling the brick with all his might) I'll kill some o' you old box-ankled niggers. (Grabs up another piece of brick.) I'm out o' your old town. Now just let some of you old half-pint Baptists let yo' wooden God and Cornstalk Jesus fool you into hittin' me. (Threatens to throw again. There are some frightened screams and the mob is heard running back.) I'm glad I'm out o' yo' ole town anyhow. I ain't never comin' back no mo', neither. You ole ugly-rump niggers done ruint de town anyhow.

(There is complete silence off stage. JIM walks a few steps with his coat and guitar, then sits down on the railroad embankment facing the audience. He pulls off one shoe and pours the sand out.

He holds the shoe in his hand a moment and looks wistfully back down the railroad track.)

JIM.

Lawd, folks sho is deceitful. (He puts on the shoe and looks back down the track again.) I never woulda thought people woulda acted like that. (Laces up the shoe) Specially Dave Carter, much as me and him done progue'd 'round together goin' in swimmin' an' playin' ball an' serenadin' de girls an' de white folks. (He sits there gloomily silent for awhile, then looks behind him and picks up his guitar and begins to pick a tune. The music is very sad, but he trails off into, "YOU MAY LEAVE AN' GO TO HALIMUHFACKS, BUT MY SLOW DRAG WILL BRING YOU BACK." When he finishes he looks at the sun and picks up his coat.)

JIM.

Reckon I better git on down de road and git some where. Lawd knows where. (Stops suddenly in his tracks and turns back toward the village. Takes a step or two.) All dat mess and stink for nothin'. Dave know good an' well I didn't meant to hurt him much. (He takes off his cap and scratches his head thoroughly. Then turns again and starts on down the road left. Enter DAISY, left, walking fast and panting, her head down. They meet.)

DAISY.

Oh, hello, Jim. (A little surprised and startled)

JIM.

(Not expecting her) Hello, Daisy. (Embarrassed silence.)

DAISY.

I was just coming over town to see how you come out.

JIM.

You don't have to go way over there to find dat out ... you and Dave done got me run outa town for nothin'.

DAISY.

(Putting her hand on his arm) Dey didn't run you outa town, did dey?

JIM.

(Shaking her hand off) Whut you reckon I'm countin' Mr. Railroad's ties for ... just to find out how many ties between here and Orlando?

DAISY.

(Hand on his arm again) Dey cain't run you off like dat!

JIM.

Take yo' hands off me, Daisy! How come they cain't run me off wid you and Dave an' ... everybody 'ginst me?

DAISY.

I ain't opened my mouf 'gainst you, Jim. I ain't said one word ... I wasn't even at de old trial. My madame wouldn't let me git off. I wuz just comin' to see 'bout you now.

JIM.

Aw, go 'head on. You figgered I was gone too long to talk about. You was haulin' it over to town to see Dave ... dat's whut you was doin' ... after gittin' me all messed up.

DAISY.

(Making as if to cry) I wasn't studyin' 'bout no Dave.

JIM.

(Hopefully) Aw, don't tell me. (Sings) Ashes to ashes, dust to dust, show me a woman that a man can trust. (DAISY is crying now.)

JIM.

What you crying for? You know you love Dave. I'm yo' monkey-man. He always could do more wid you that I could.

DAISY.

Naw, you ain't no monkey-man neither. I don't want you to leave town. I didn't want y'all to be fightin' over me, nohow.

JIM.

Aw, rock on down de road wid dat stuff. A two-timin' cloaker like you don't keer whut come off. Me and Dave been good friends ever since we was born till you had to go flouncing yourself around.

DAISY.

What did I do? All I did was to come over town to see you and git a mouf-ful of gum. Next thing I know y'all is fighting and carrying on.

JrM: (Stands silent for a while) Did you come over there Sat'-day night to see me sho nuff, sugar babe?

DAISY.

Everybody could see dat but you.

JIM.

Just like I told you, Daisy, before you ever left from round here and went up North. I could kiss you every day ... just as regular as pig-tracks.

DAISY.

And I tole you I could stand it too—just as regular as you could.

JIM.

(Catching her by the arm and pulling her down with him onto the rail) Set down, here, Daisy. Less talk some chat. You want me sho nuff? Hones' to God?

DAISY.

(Coyly) 'Member whut I told you out on de lake last summer?

JIM.

Sho nuff, Daisy? (DAISY nods smilingly)

JIM.

(Sadly) But I got to go 'way. Whut we gointer do 'bout dat?

DAISY.

Where you goin', Jim?

JIM.

(Looking sadly down the track) God knows.

(Off stage from the same direction from which JIM entered comes the sound of whistling and tramping of feet on the ties.)

JIM.

(Brightening) Dat's Dave! (Frowning) Wonder whut he doin' walkin' dis track? (Looks accusingly at DAISY) I bet he's goin' to yo' work-place.

DAISY.

Whut for?

JIM.

He ain't goin' to see de madame—must be goin' to see you. (He starts to rise petulantly as DAVE comes upon the scene. Daisy rises also.)

DAVE.

(Looks accusingly from one to the other) Whut y'all jumpin' up for? I . . .

JIM.

Whut you gut to do wid us business? Tain't none of yo' business if we stand up, set down or fly like a skeeter hawk.

DAVE.

Who said I keered? Dis railroad belongs to de man—I kin walk it good as you, cain't I?

JIM.

(Laughing exultantly) Oh, yeah, Mr. Do-Dirty! You figgered you had done run me on off so you could git Daisy all by yo'self. You was headin' right for her work-place.

DAVE.

I wasn't no such a thing.

JIM.

You was. Didn't I hear you coming down de track all whistling and everything?

DAVE.

Youse a big ole Georgy-something-ain't-so! I done got my belly full of Daisy Sat'day night. She can't snore in my ear no more.

DAISY.

(Indignantly) Whut you come here low-ratin' me for, Dave Carter? I ain't done nothin' to you but treat you white. Who come rubbed yo' ole head for you yestiddy if it wasn't me?

DAVE.

Yeah, you rubbed my head all right, and I lakted dat. But everybody say you done toted a pan to Joe Clarke's barn for Jim before I seen you.

DAISY.

Think I was going to let Jim lay there 'thout nothing fitten for a dog to eat?

DAVE.

That's all right, Daisy. If you want to pay Jim for knockin' me in de head, all right. But I'm a man in a class ... in a class to myself and nobody knows my name.

JIM.

(Snatching Daisy around to face him) Was you over to Dave's house yestiddy rubbing his ole head and cloaking wid him to run me outa town ... and me looked up in dat barn wid de cows and mules?

DAISY.

(Sobbing) All both of y'all hollerin' at me an' fussin' me just cause I tries to be nice... and neither one of y'all don't keer nothin' bout me.

(BOTH BOYS glare at each other over DAISY's head and both try to hug her at the same time. She violently wrenches herself away from both and makes as if to move on.)

DAISY.

Leave me go! Take yo' rusty pams offen me. I'm going on back to my work-place. I just got off to see bout y'all and look how y'all treat me.

JIM.

Wait a minute, Daisy. I love you like God loves Gabriel ... and dat's His best angel.

DAVE.

Daisy, I love you harder than de thunder can bump a sump ... if I don't ... God's a gopher.

DAISY.

(Brightening) Dat's de first time you ever said so.

DAVE & JIM.

Who?

JIM.

Whut you hollering "Who" for? Yo' fat don't fit no limb.

DAVE.

Speak when you spoken to ... come when you called, next fall you'll be my coon houn' dog.

JIM.

Table dat discussion. (Turning to DAISY) You ain't never give me no chance to talk wid you right.

DAVE.

YOU made me feel like you was trying to put de Ned book on me all de time. Do you love me sho nuff, Daisy?

DAISY.

(Blooming again into coquetry) Aw, y'all better stop dat. You know you don't mean it.

DAVE.

Who don't mean it? Lemme tell you something, mama, if you

was mine I wouldn't have you counting no ties wid yo' pretty lil toes. Know whut I'd do?

DAISY.

(Coyly) Naw, whut would you do?

DAVE.

I'd buy you a whole passenger train ... and hire some mens to run it for you.

DAISY.

(Happily) Oo-ooh, Dave.

JIM.

(To Dave) De wind may blow, de doorway slam

Dat shut you shootin' ain't worth a dam.

(To Daisy)

I'd buy you a great big ole ship ... and then, baby, I'd buy you a ocean to sail yo' ship on.

Daisy: (Happily) Oo-ooh, Jim.

DAVE.

(To Jim; A long tain, a short caboose

Dat lie whut you shootin', ain't no use.

(To Daisy)

Miss Daisy, know what I'd do for you?

DAISY.

Naw, whut?

DAVE.

I'd come down de river riding a mud cat and loading a minnow.

DAISY.

Lawd, Dave, you sho is propaganda.

JIM.

(Peevishly) Naw he ain't ... he's just lying ... he's a noble liar. Know whut I'd do if you was mine?

DAISY.

Naw, Jim.

JIM.

I'd make a panther wash yl' dishes and a 'gater chop yo' wood for you.

DAVE.

Daisy, how come you let Jim lie lak dat? He's as big as a liar as he is a man. But sho nuff now, laying all sides to jokes, Jim there don't even know how to answer you. If you don't b'lieve it ... ast him something.

DAISY.

(To Jim) You like me much, Jim?

JIM.

(Enthusiastically) Yeah, Daisy I sho do.

DAVE.

(Triumphant) See dat! I tole you he didn't know how to answer nobody like you. If he was talking to some of them ol' funny looking gals over town he'd be answering 'em just right. But he got to learn how to answer you. Now you ast me something and see how I answer you.

DAISY.

Do you like me, Dave?

DAVE.

(Very properly in a falsetto voice) Yes ma'am! Dat's de way to answer swell folks like you. Furthermore, less we prove which one of us love you do best right now. (To JIM) Jim, how much time would you do on de chain-gang for dis 'oman?

JIM.

Twenty years and like it.

DAVE.

See dat, Daisy? Dat nigger ain't willin' to do no time for you. I'd beg de judge to gimme life. (Both JIM and DAVE laugh)

DAISY.

Y'all doin' all dis bookooin' out here on de railroad track but I bet y'all crazy 'bout Bootsie and Teets and a whole heap of other gals.

JIM.

Cross my feet and hope to die! I'd ruther see all de other wimmen folks in de worl' dead than for you to have de toothache.

DAVE.

If I was dead and any other woman come near my coffin de undertaker would have to do his job all over ... 'cause I'd git right up and walk off. Furthermore, Miss Daisy, ma'am, also ma'am, which would you ruther be a lark a flying or a dove a settin' ... ma'am, also ma'am?

DAISY.

'Course I'd ruther be a dove.

JIM.

Miss Daisy, ma'am, also ma'am ... if you marry dis nigger over my head, I'm going to git me a green hickory club and season it over yo' head.

DAVE.

Don't you be skeered, baby ... papa kin take keer a you. (To Jim) Countin' from de finger (Suiting the action to the word) back to de thumb ... start anything I got you some.

JIM.

Aw, I don't want no more fight wid you, Dave.

DAVE.

Who said anything about fighting? We just provin' who love Daisy de best. (To DAISY) Now, which one of us you think love you de best?

DAISY.

Deed I don't know, Dave.

DAVE.

Baby, I'd walk de water for you ... and tote a mountain on my head while I'm walkin'.

JIM.

Know what I'd do, honey babe? If you was a thousand miles from home and you didn't have no ready-made money and you had to walk all de way, walkin' till ye' feet start to rolling, just like a wheel, and I was riding way up in de sky, I'd step backwards offa dat aryplane just to walk home wid you.

DAISY.

(Falling on JIM's neck) Jim, when you talk to me like dat I just can't stand it. Less us git married right now.

JIM.

Now you talkin' like a blue-back speller. Less go!

DAVE.

(Sadly) You gointer leave me lak dis, Daisy?

DAISY.

(Sadly) I likes you, too, Dave, I sho do. But I can't marry both of y'all at de same time.

JIM.

Aw, come on, Daisy ... sun's gettin' low. (He starts off pulling DAISY)

DAVE: Whut's I'm gointer do? (Walking after them)

JIM.

Gwan back and dance ... you make out you don't need me to play none.

DAVE.

(Almost tearfully) Aw, Jim, shucks! Where y'all going?

(DAISY comes to an abrupt halt and stops JIM)

Daisy: That's right, honey. Where is we goin' sho nuff?

JIM.

(Sadly) Deed I don't know, baby. They just sentenced me to go ... they didn't say where and I don't know.

DAISY.

How we goin' nohow to go when we don't know where we goin'?

(JIM looks at DAVE as if he expects some help but DAVE stands sadly silent. JIM takes a few steps forward as if to go on. DAISY makes a step or two, unwillingly, then looks behind her and stops. DAVE looks as if he will follow them.)

DAISY.

Jim! (He stops and turns) Wait a minute! Whut we gointer do when we git there?

JIM.

Where?

DAISY.

Where we goin'?

JIM.

I done tole you I don't know where it is.

DAISY.

But how we gointer git something to eat and a place to stay?

JIM.

Play and dance ... just like I been doin'.

DAISY.

You can't dance and Dave ain't gointer be ther.

JIM.

(Looks appealingly at DAVE, then away quickly) Well, I can't help dat, can I?

DAISY.

(Brightly) I tell you whut, Jim! Less us don't go nowhere. They sentenced you to leave Eatonville and youse more than a mile from de city limits already. Youse in Maitland now. Supposin' you come live on de white folks' place wid me after we git married. Eatonville ain't got nothin' to do wid you livin' in Maitland.

JIM.

Dat'a a good idea, Daisy.

DAISY.

(Jumping into his arms) And listen, honey, you don't have to be beholden to Dave nor nobody else. You can throw dat ole box away if you want to. I know ehre you can get a swell job.

JIM.

(Sheepishly) Doin' whut? (Looks lovingly at his guitar)

DAISY.

(Almost dancing) Yard man. All you have to do is wash windows, and sweep de sidewalk, and scrub off de steps and porch and hoe up de weeds and rake up de leaves and dig a few holes now and then with a spade ... to plant some trees and things like that. It's a good steady job.

JIM.

(After a long deliberation) You see, Daisy, de Mayor and corporation told me to go on off and I oughter go.

DAISY.

Well, I'm not going tippin' down no railroad track like a Maltese cat. I wasn't brought up knockin' round from here to yonder.

JIM.

Well, I wasn't brought up wid no spade in my hand ... and ain't going to start it now.

DAISY.

But sweetheart, we got to live, ain't we? We got to git hold of money before we kin do anything. I don't mean to stay in de white folks' kitchen all my days.

JIM.

Yeah, all dat's true, but you couldn't buy a flea a waltzing jacket wid de money I'm going to make wid a hoe and spade.

DAISY.

(Getting tearful) You don't want me. You don't love me.

JIM.

Yes, I do, darling, I love you. Youse de one letting a spade come between us. (HE caresses her) I loves you and you only. You don't see me dragging a whole gang of farming tools into us business, do you?

DAISY.

(Stiffly) Well, I ain't going to marry no man that ain't going to work and take care of me.

JIM.

I don't mind working if de job ain't too heavy for me. I ain't going to bother wid nothin' in my hands heavier than dis box ... and I totes it round my neck 'most of de time.

(DAISY makes a despairing gesture as JIM takes a step or two away from her. She turns to DAVE finally.)

DAISY.

Well, I reckon you loves me the best anyhow. You wouldn't talk to me like Jim did, would you, Dave?

DAVE.

Naw, I wouldn't say what he said a-tall.

DAISY.

(Cuddling up to him) Whut would you say, honey?

DAVE.

I'd say dat box was too heavy for me to fool wid. I wouldn't tote nothing heavier than my hat and I feel like I'm 'busing myself sometime totin' dat.

DAISY.

(Outraged) Don't you mean to work none?

DAVE.

Wouldn't hit a lick at a snake.

DAISY.

I don't blame you, Dave (Looks down at his feet) cause toting dem feet of yourn is enough to break down your constitution.

JIM.

(Airily) That's all right ... dem foots done put plenty bread in our moufs.

DAVE.

Not by they selves though ... wid de help of dat box, Jim. When you gits having fits on dat box, boy, my foots has hysterics. Daisy, you marry Jim cause I don't want to come between y'all. He's my buddy.

JIM.

Come to think of it, Dave, she was yourn first. You take and handle dat spade for her.

DAVE.

You heard her say it is all I can do to lift up dese feets and put 'em down. Where I'm going to git any time to wrassle wid any hoes and shovels? You kin git round better'n me. You done won Daisy ... I give in. I ain't going to bite no fren' of mine in de back.

DAISY.

Both of you niggers can git yo' hat an' yo' heads and git on down de road. Neither one of y'all don't have to have me. I got a good job and plenty men beggin for yo' chance.

JIM.

Dat's right, Daisy, you go git you one them mens whut don't mind smelling mules ... and beating de white folks to de barn every morning. I don't wanta be bothered wid nothin' but dis box.

DAVE.

And I can't strain wid nothin' but my feets.

(DAISY walks slowly away in the direction from which she came. Both watch her a little wistfully for a minute. The sun is setting.)

DAVE.

Guess I better be gittin' on back ... it's most dark. Where you goin' Jim?

JIM.

I don't know, Dave. Down de road, I reckon.

DAVE.

Whyncher come on back to town. 'Tain't no use you proguein' up and down de railroad track when you got a home.

JIM.

They done lawed me way from it for hittin' you wid dat bone.

DAVE.

Dat ain't nothin'. It was my head you hit. An' if I don't keer whut dem old ugly-rump niggers got to do wid it?

JIM.

They might not let me come in town.

DAVE.

(Seizing JIM's arm and facing him back toward the town) They better! Look here, Jim, if they try to keep you out dat town we'll go out to dat swamp and git us a mule bone a piece and come into town and boil dat stew down to a low gravy.

JIM.

You mean dat, Dave? (DAVE nods his head eagerly) Us wasn't mad wid one 'nother nohow. (Beligerently) Come on, less go back to town. Dem mallet-heads better leave me be, too. (Picks up a heavy stick) I wish Lum would come tellin' me 'bout de law when I got all dis law in my hands. And de rest o' dem gator-faced jigs, if they ain't got a whole sto' o' mule bones and a good determination, they better not bring no mess up. Come on, boy.

(THEY start back together toward town, JIM picking a dance tune on his guitar, and DAVE cutting steps on the ties beside him, singing, prancing and happily, they exit, right, as

THE CURTAIN FALLS.)

www.ingramcontent.com/pod-product-compliance
Lightning Source LLC
LaVergne TN
LVHW021538080426
835509LV00019B/2712